leader's

CHOOSE THE LIFE

EXPLORING
A FAITH
THAT EMBRACES
DISCIPLESHIP

Bill Hull
and
Paul Mascarella

Discipleship Inside Out™

NavPress is the publishing ministry of The Navigators, an international Christian organization and leader in personal spiritual development. NavPress is committed to helping people grow spiritually and enjoy lives of meaning and hope through personal and group resources that are biblically rooted, culturally relevant, and highly practical.

**For a free catalog go to www.NavPress.com
or call 1.800.366.7788 in the United States or 1.800.839.4769 in Canada.**

© 2010 by Bill Hull

All rights reserved. No part of this publication may be reproduced in any form without written permission from NavPress, P.O. Box 35001, Colorado Springs, CO 80935. www.navpress.com

NAVPRESS and the NAVPRESS logo are registered trademarks of NavPress. Absence of ® in connection with marks of NavPress or other parties does not indicate an absence of registration of those marks.

ISBN-13: 978-1-61521-570-6

Printed in the United States of America

1 2 3 4 5 6 7 8 / 14 13 12 11 10

CONTENTS

Introduction 5

About the Guide 7

Preparing for the First Meeting 13

Week One:
   Your First Community Meeting 15

Week Two:
   How I Got to This Point 17

Week Three:
   The Need for the Life 29

Week Four:
   The Call to the Life 41

Week Five:
   The Habits of the Life 53

Week Six:
   The Inner Workings of the Life 66

Week Seven:
   The Mind and the Life 77

Week Eight:
   Relationships and the Life 89

Week Nine:
   Submission and the Life 101

Week Ten:
   Leadership and the Life 113

Appendix	125
Leader's Guide	127
Notes	158
About the Authors	159
Other Books by Bill Hull	160

INTRODUCTION

To choose the life is to commit to a way or pattern of life. Its basis is humility and it is a life of self-denial and submission to others. We choose it because Christ chose it for Himself. The essence of faith is to take up our cross daily and follow Him.

We don't just amble our way into this pattern; it is a conscious decision to live by faith. It is fundamentally about giving up the right to run our own lives. It is the life Jesus lived, the life to which He has called every disciple. It means to be as unnecessary and irrelevant to our culture as He was to His. And just as we are never more alive as when we deny ourselves, we are never more relevant and necessary than when we choose His life.

The life that Jesus lived and prescribed for us is different from the one being offered by many churches. His servant leadership was radically distinct from what is extolled by secular society and even too bold for what is modeled in the Christian community.

Henri Nouwen said it well: "The long painful history of the Church is people ever and again tempted to choose power over love, control over the cross, being a leader over being led."[1] It is as Dietrich Bonhoeffer said: "Christianity without discipleship is always Christianity without Christ."[2]

What will we choose? Will we surrender to the powerful forces of our culture and simply try to be successful for Jesus? Or will we choose the life that Jesus chose and commit to following Him regardless of where He leads?

To put it another way, to choose the life is to commit to:

- Believing as Jesus believed
- Living as Jesus lived

- Loving as Jesus loved
- Ministering as Jesus ministered
- Leading as Jesus led

To choose the life is to choose *His* life. Jesus *chose* His life.

Because we come out of a divine nature, which chooses to be divine, we must choose to be divine, to be of God, to be one with God, loving and living as he loves and lives. . . . Man cannot originate this life; it must be shown him, and he must choose it. . . . We are not and cannot become true sons without our will willing his will, our doing following his making. He was not the Son of God because he could not help it, but because he willed to be.

— GEORGE MACDONALD

Every time you make a choice you are turning the central part of you into something different than it was before. . . . Each of us at that moment is progressing to one state or another.

— C. S. LEWIS

The ills of the church and of the individual almost totally derive from the simple failure to just do what Jesus told us to do in the Great Commission. That is what it means to choose the life. There is no excuse whatsoever for not doing it, and every rationalization is simply a wound to our own soul, an injury to our group, and an insult to the Christ who told us what to do.

— DALLAS WILLARD

ABOUT THE *GUIDE*

Its Purpose

Bill Hull's book *Choose the Life* exists to assist the motivated disciple in entering into a more profound way of thinking and living. That way is the pattern of life Jesus modeled and then called every interested person to follow. It is a life grounded in humility, characterized by submission, obedience, suffering, and the joys of exaltation. It is the life that transforms its adherents and penetrates the strongest resistance.

Choose the Life challenges traditional thinking about what it means to be a Christian; it rebuilds the gospel from the disciple up. It asks what is wrong with the gospel taught in contemporary Western culture and suggests some changes in the way it is communicated by the church. It then calls upon each person to rethink what it means to be a follower of Jesus.

A Disciple's Guide to Choose the Life is designed to lead disciples in a ten-week course through *Choose the Life*. However, it is more than simply a reading guide. It presents the ideas in *Choose the Life* so as to provoke a disciple's thinking toward the application of these truths, which produces in him a faith hospitable to healthy spiritual growth — a faith that embraces discipleship.

Its Participants

Virtually all significant change can, should be, and eventually is tested in relationship to others. To say that one is more loving without it being verified in relation to others is hollow. Not only do others need to be involved to test one's progress, they are needed to encourage and help one another in the journey of transformation. Therefore, going on the journey with others is absolutely necessary.

The *Guide* is designed to lead each disciple in a personal journey of spiritual formation by his participation within a "Community" of disciples, who have likewise decided to choose the life.

The "Community" is composed of (optimally) two to six disciples being led through this ten-week exploration of *Choose the Life*.

Participants in the Community will have agreed to make time to perform the daily assignments as directed by the *Guide*. They have agreed to pray daily for the other members of their Community and keep whatever is shared at their "Community Meeting" in complete confidence (unless express permission to disclose a specific matter is given by all involved). They will attend and fully participate in each weekly Community Meeting.

Its Process

Change is a process. Events can change people, but most often transformation is a process that takes time. Most studies on change agree that acquiring a new idea and putting it into practice so that it becomes permanent requires three months. This would be the minimum time required. The ten weeks to finish the *Guide* provide solid opportunity for significant transformation. The process employed by the *Guide* includes:

- Reading the Scripture together
- Reading a common philosophy of the Christian experience
- Journaling insights, questions, and prayers
- Discussion over material that has already been studied, prayed over, and reflected upon
- Helping each other keep one's commitment to God
- Helping each other break free of areas of defeat and bondage
- A common commitment to apply what God has impressed on each member
- A common commitment to impact those with whom members have contact

Its Pattern

The *Guide* leads an exploration of each successive chapter of the book (including the introductory material) in ten weeks. Each week, beginning with chapter 1, a chapter is explored in five daily thirty-minute sessions.

At each daily session, the disciple begins with prayer focused on the issues to be presented in the daily reading. The daily reading provides each disciple with core thoughts and key ideas that will be explored in the day's exercises. Provided questions are designed to help the disciples' understanding of the core thoughts and key ideas. Disciples are then directed to reflect on the application of these core thoughts and key ideas to their own spiritual growth. Journaling space is provided for answering questions and recording the thoughts, questions, applications, and insights stemming from reflection.

Once weekly (at the sixth session), the disciples meets with the other disciples, comprising the "Community" at their Community Meeting. Here they pray together, discuss the core thoughts and key ideas introduced in the week's readings, share from their times of reflection, and encourage each other on their journeys.

Although the *Guide* was designed primarily for use by groups consisting of two to six members, the material contained within can easily be used to lead much larger groups in a discussion-based exploration of *Choose the Life*. This is done by using the ten weekly Community Meetings as the agendas for a ten-week discussion program. It is recommended that the accompanying DVD be used to introduce the topic for the week's discussion. Additional questions to enhance the weekly meeting may be gleaned from the week's five-day study program.

Lastly, it is recommended that the leader (or leaders) of a weekly discussion group proceed through the *Guide* together as their own Community group. The insights they will acquire by proceeding on their own journey through *Choose the Life* will be invaluable to them and the larger group they will be leading.

When leading a classroom-sized (or larger) group through *Choose the Life*, one must keep in mind that most of the "spiritual traction" for transformation is due to the interaction that the Lord has with each individual as He interacts with him or her through the other individuals in a community of believers. To preserve this traction, the leader must provide a venue and time for this interaction. For this reason, it is suggested that some time during the weekly session the leader divide the large group into smaller groups (mimicking the two-to-six-member Community group) for the purpose of more intimately discussing the issues presented in the week's session. It is reported that after experiencing successive weeks with the same members of this smaller discussion group, individuals previously not participants in a small group program have desired to continue in just such a program.

While the authors believe that the most effective and efficient means of leading individuals to healthy spiritual transformation is in the context of a smaller Community group, we do acknowledge that the larger group setting may be the only means currently available to a church's leadership whereby the biblical truths taught in *Choose the Life* are likely to be made available. We believe most strongly that although the form of instruction is important, the function is what must be preserved: *verum supremus vultus* (truth above form).

Its Product

Learning studies demonstrate the importance of application. The most relevant question a teacher can ask is, "Are my students learning?" According to a leading learning researcher, people remember:

- Ten percent of what they read
- Twenty percent of what they hear
- Thirty percent of what they see
- Fifty percent of what they see and hear
- Seventy percent of what they say
- Ninety-five percent of what they teach someone else[3]

Each session asks the disciples to determine what concrete activity they can take that week to apply what they have learned. The *Guide* highly values the spiritual traction one can get by facing challenges in a high-trust community. This avoids the hothouse effect (people not experienced in the reality of ministry) on groups that do not answer the challenge to reach beyond themselves.

Christ was a man for others; disciples, then, are to be people for others. It is only in losing ourselves in the mission of loving others that we live in balance and experience the joy that Christ has promised. This is the faith that embraces discipleship. This is the life that cultivates Christlikeness, the only life of faith worthy enough to justify our calling upon others to choose the life.

PREPARING FOR THE FIRST MEETING

Community

The first order of business is to determine the members, size, and makeup of the Community.

The Community should consist of:

- **Members**
  All believers
  No particular age range or level of spiritual maturity (or Christian experience) should be the overarching criterion for inclusion in your Community, but given that the objectives of *Choose the Life* are obtainable only by Christians, it is assumed that each member of any particular *Choose the Life* Community is already a Christian.

- **Makeup**
  Two to six members (optimally)
  The *Guide* can also be used as a discussion guide for leading larger groups through an exploration of *Choose the Life*.

- **Materials**
  The book, guide, and leader's guide with DVD
  Once the membership of the Community is established, each member should acquire a copy of the book, *Choose the Life: Exploring a Faith That Embraces Discipleship*, and the course guide, *A Disciple's Guide to Choose the Life*. In addition, the leader needs to acquire the course leader's guide with DVD. The DVD features Bill Hull, the author of

Choose the Life, introducing each week's core thought, key ideas, and concepts. These materials must be available to each member at least one week prior to the first Community Meeting.

This brings us to the second order of business: when and where the Community will meet.

CALENDAR

The members of the Community need to establish when and where the Community will have its weekly meetings. Bear in mind that it will require about ninety minutes from start to finish to accomplish all that is to be done at the Community Meeting. What matters most in the time set for these meetings is that all of the members are able to make this accommodation. As you will learn in the course of this journey, the commitment to Community is essential to your own personal transformation. Therefore, it is imperative that all members be present and able to contribute each time the Community meets.

In selecting the location of your meeting, choose a site that will allow for confidential conversation, ease of access, and the fewest possible interruptions.

COMMITMENT

Having determined the Community's membership and meeting location and time, the members of the newly formed Community need to clearly state and affirm their commitment to accomplishing what is stated in their Purpose and Covenant. We have included a covenant, located in the appendix. Each member should read, sign, and turn in the covenant at the first Community Meeting.

The final order of business in preparation for your first Community Meeting is for each Community member to read Dallas Willard's foreword to *Choose the Life* (pages 6–8) and the preface, "A Conversation Starter" (pages 9–14), and then write their answers for each of the questions posed in the *Guide* for the first week's Community Meeting.

WEEK 1

Your First Community Meeting

In preparation for this meeting, all Community members will have read Dallas Willard's foreword (pages 6–8) and preface, "A Conversation Starter" (pages 9–14), from *Choose the Life* and have written their answers to each of the questions posed in the *Guide* for the first week's Community Meeting.

Questions
1. When you were a child, to what were you highly committed? Describe what that commitment entailed and how it affected your commitments as an adult.

2. Dallas Willard cites three things vital to spiritual growth (pages 6–7). Discuss each one and evaluate its place in your present experience.

3. What does Bonhoeffer mean by "cheap grace" (page 10)? Do you think "cheap grace" is a problem in your life, faith community, or church? How is it manifested?

4. Do you agree with the description of the "problem" and the "solution" advanced (pages 11–13)?

Reflection
Talk with one another about your readiness (or reluctance), at this time, to choose the life—specifically, about living out "a faith that embraces discipleship." Why now?

Acts 19:1-10

Prayer
Share matters for the Community to pray about throughout the following week. Make note of the requests made to use in your daily time of prayer.

Caleb, Coly → School/Career Direction Encourage + Discipline Rel'nshp - Chloe + Family

Rose - Dizziness... Margaret - Healing...

Close
Pray together to close the meeting.

Angie - Interview coming up 10/1

> *Choose the Life*, **Chapter One**
> **"HOW I GOT TO THIS POINT"**

WEEK TWO

DAY ONE

Prayer
Dear Lord, help me to be dissatisfied with my current ways of being "successful" in accomplishing Your calling in my life. Begin now to develop in me a taste for Your ways.

Today's Reading
Choose the Life, chapter 1 (pages 15–16)

Question
What were the signs that indicated to the author that something was "not working," that something was wrong?

Reflection
What has been the greatest motivator for change in your life? Why was it so motivating for you?

Prayer
Pray for each member of your Community and their shared requests.

DAY TWO

Prayer
Lord, today help me to be very conscious of how I conduct myself. Help me to see if I exhibit character traits that those who know Jesus well would recognize.

Today's Reading
Choose the Life, chapter 1 (page 17, paragraphs 1–4)

Question
What caused the author to want to change? What were the factors that were causing the despair the author was feeling?

Reflection
Do you find yourself "stuck in the same rut" of "religious activity without transformation" and "doing things right" but with "little movement from the Spirit"? List those things you are doing "right." What do you expect to see in those things which would evidence the Spirit's movement?

Things I'm doing right	Expected evidence of the Spirit's movement

Prayer
Pray for each member of your Community and their shared requests.

DAY THREE

Prayer
Lord, help me to admit my failure in following You. Help me to gain a greater understanding of Your love and acceptance of me as I seek to be transformed into the disciple You've called me to be.

Today's Reading
Choose the Life, chapter 1 (page 17, paragraph 5, through page 18, paragraph 2)

Questions
1. What caused the "plague" to lift?

2. What did the author mean when he told his congregation that he intended to "evangelism them"?

Reflection
What do you believe you should see happening in your life if you were truly living as a disciple of Jesus?

Prayer
Pray for each member of your Community and their shared requests.

DAY FOUR

Prayer
Lord, help me to change my understanding of following You so that I really act like the disciple You describe in the Sermon on the Mount.

Today's Reading
Choose the Life, chapter 1 (page 18, paragraph 3, through page 19, paragraph 3)

Questions
1. According to the author, what is the "problem" and what is the "solution"?

2. What does a disciple look like (according to Matthew 5–7)?

Reflection
How (and about what) have you been practicing "sin management"?

Prayer
Pray for each member of your Community and their shared requests.

DAY FIVE

Prayer
Lord, teach me how to minister as You minister and lead others the way You lead.

Today's Reading
Choose the Life, chapter 1 (page 19, paragraph 4, through page 21)

Question
What do you suppose the author means when he states that "Jesus was irrelevant and unnecessary to His culture"?

Reflection
What are the obstacles that keep you from sincerely saying to God, "Lord, I'm not afraid of any change You want to make in my life"? List the obstacles and list what fear they cause you to have.

The Obstacles	The Fear

Prayer
Pray for each member of your Community and their shared requests.

> *Choose the Life*, **Chapter One**
> **"HOW I GOT TO THIS POINT"**

WEEK TWO

Community Meeting

DAY SIX

In preparation for this week's meeting, you will have read chapter 1, "How I Got to This Point," in *Choose the Life* and have answered the reading questions for each day.

As a group, answer the following questions.

Questions
1. What did the author mean when he used the metaphor of "fly-fishing on ice" to represent his struggles while serving as senior pastor at a "successful" church?

2. What are the differences between believing in Jesus and believing what Jesus believed (pages 19–20)?

Discuss the fivefold way the author presents of how we are to follow Jesus (pages 19–20).

Reflection
1. What are we to understand by the author's statement that "competence is a cul-de-sac"?

2. How are brokenness and humility "essential to spiritual health"?

Close
Share matters for the Community to pray about throughout the following week. Pray to close the meeting.

> *Jesus calls us not to sin management but to transformation, where we experience one breakthrough after another and do away with sin in our lives.*

> *Choose the Life*, **Chapter Two**
> **"THE NEED FOR THE LIFE"**

WEEK THREE

DAY ONE

Prayer
Lord, teach me to repent of my commitment to a non-discipleship style of Christianity.

Today's Reading
Choose the Life, chapter 2 (page 23 through page 28, paragraph 2)

Questions
1. What does the author mean when he says that "we have made the test for salvation doctrinal rather than behavioral"?

2. What is "missing" from the gospel of our modern church?

Reflection
What are your "default settings," where did you get them, and why do you keep them?

Prayer
Pray for each member of your Community and their shared requests.

DAY TWO

Prayer
Lord, remake me into someone who is neither bored nor boring.

Today's Reading
Choose the Life, chapter 2 (page 28, paragraph 3, through page 31, paragraph 2)

Questions
1. Do you agree with the author that "discipleship or spiritual formation is the primary and exclusive work of the church"? Why is this understanding correct or incorrect?

2. Why has church become "boring"?

Reflection
Given the truth of Luke 6:40, why would being like Jesus keep you from ever being a bored or boring person?

Prayer
Pray for each member of your Community and their shared requests.

DAY THREE

Prayer
Lord, help me not to fear Your leading. Help me to make heart-deep commitments to You.

Today's Reading
Choose the Life, chapter 2 (page 31, paragraph 3, through page 35, paragraph 2)

Questions
1. What is different in the first disciples' understanding of discipleship from the contemporary church's understanding?

2. What does the author say is the first thing that must be done?

Reflection
Reflect on the idea of "choosing the life" in light of Matthew 6:24.

Prayer
Pray for each member of your Community and their shared requests.

DAY FOUR

Prayer
Lord, help me to submit to Your leading through "another like-minded person in mutual submission and humility." Help me not to fear bringing "everything out of hiding and into the light."

Today's Reading
Choose the Life, chapter 2 (page 35, paragraph 3, through page 40, paragraph 3)

Questions
1. What is the "key part of being a follower of Jesus" (page 35)?

2. What should discipleship look like today (page 36)?

Reflection
If faith is real only in obedience, how would the casual observer recognize that you have this faith? How do those who know you best "see" your faith?

Prayer
Pray for each member of your Community and their shared requests.

DAY FIVE

Prayer
Lord, prepare me to understand and make the changes I need to make to become Your disciple and to make disciples for You among the unbelieving.

Today's Reading
Choose the Life, chapter 2 (page 50, paragraph 4, through page 42)

Questions
1. What does this "new kind of evangelism" consist of?

2. What is "the great omission in the Great Commission"? What has this "omission" caused?

Reflection
About what particular sin have you "raised the white flag of surrender" and chosen the "sin management" approach to addressing it?

Prayer
Pray for each member of your Community and their shared requests.

Choose the Life, **Chapter Two**
"THE NEED FOR THE LIFE"

WEEK THREE

Community Meeting

DAY SIX

In preparation for this week's Meeting, you will have read chapter 2, "The Need for the Life," in *Choose the Life* and have answered the reading questions for each day.

As a group, answer the following questions.

Questions
1. Discuss whether your test for salvation has been primarily "doctrinal" rather than "behavioral."

2. Discuss the statement that "faith is only real in obedience." How does it challenge our modern notion of faith (page 24)?

3. How does holding a faith that does not transform lead to "sin management" (page 26)?

Reflection
Do you think your church and other churches have accepted a non-discipleship Christianity? Is it optional in your life? Do you think you have a choice (pages 26–30)?

Close
Share matters for the Community to pray about throughout the following week. Pray to close the meeting.

> *Discipleship today must also begin with a commitment of submission to at least one other person. Choosing the life begins right here.*

> *Choose the Life*, **Chapter Three**
> **"THE CALL TO THE LIFE"**

WEEK FOUR

DAY ONE

Prayer
Lord, help me to understand exactly what it is that You are calling me to do. Enable me to do it and then allow me to lead others in it.

Today's Reading
Choose the Life, chapter 3 (pages 43–47)

Questions
1. What does the author mean by "the first act of a disciple is obedience, not a confession"?

2. How, in our current church culture, is "spiritual greatness" being "measured by size"?

Reflection
What are some of the rivals in your life to following Jesus?

Prayer
Pray for each member of your Community and their shared requests.

DAY TWO

Prayer
Lord, give me the strength to deny myself the right to be in charge of my own life. Train me to appreciate my new position as I follow behind You.

Today's Reading
Choose the Life, chapter 3 (page 47, paragraph 1, through page 52)

Questions
1. Who is Jesus calling to the life of discipleship? Why does the term *spiritual formation* war against the inclusion of those whom Jesus intended to include?

2. What is self-denial, and why is it "essential" (pages 49–52)?

Reflection
What are some things you must deny yourself in order to follow Jesus in the fullest sense of being His disciple?

Prayer
Pray for each member of your Community and their shared requests.

DAY THREE

Prayer
Lord, help me to give up control of the timing and method of my actions and submit my dreams, visions, and breakthrough ideas to Your leadership. I deny myself in order to say yes to You. Please steady my hand as I drive the stake of obedience to You through the heart of my will, my ego, and my desire to control.

Today's Reading
Choose the Life, chapter 3 (page 52, paragraph 1, through page 55, paragraph 1)

Question
Why is seeking the answer to the question "Lord, what do You want me to do; what is my mission?" *before* we start walking the path of obedience a common mistake?

Reflection
What do you and others who know you well identify as your strengths (page 53)?

Prayer
Pray for each member of your Community and their shared requests.

DAY FOUR

Prayer
Lord, remind me to lead not from my strengths but from a heart that is willing to suffer any humiliation as I follow Your leading.

Today's Reading
Choose the Life, chapter 3 (page 55, paragraph 1, through page 57)

Questions
1. Why does Jesus use the simile of taking up a cross in His description of following Him (see Luke 9:23)?

2. Why does Jesus tell us to take up our cross daily?

Reflection
What are the areas in which you are "following with doubt"?

Prayer
Pray for each member of your Community and their shared requests.

DAY FIVE

Prayer
Lord, teach me to do first what interests You most—often what is in my neighbor's best interest—and never what interests only me.

Today's Reading
Choose the Life, chapter 3 (page 58–60)

Questions
1. What is "God's paradox" (page 58)?

2. What are the "rewards" for answering "to the Society of Jesus"?

Reflection
How have you benefited in living by God's paradox?

Prayer
Pray for each member of your Community and their shared requests.

Choose the Life, **Chapter Three**
"THE CALL TO THE LIFE"

WEEK FOUR

Community Meeting

DAY SIX

In preparation for this week's Meeting, you will have read chapter 3, "The Call to the Life," in *Choose the Life* and have answered the reading questions for each day.

As a group, answer the following questions.

Questions
1. What is meant by "Faith is more than agreement; it is taking up your cross"?

2. The author presents various things disciples are urged to follow. These alternatives to Jesus' calling may appeal to us but can be very dangerous. What are these alternatives, and why could they lead us astray (page 46)?

Reflection

1. How should a disciple give these alternatives their proper consideration when seeking to follow Jesus' leading?

2. Why is self-denial "essential" (pages 49–52)?

Close

Share matters for the Community to pray about throughout the following week. Pray to close the meeting.

> *Until we actually step out in obedience to Him, we can't experience the transformation of our character. As we follow Him, Jesus will reveal more about Himself and our mission day by day.*

Choose the Life, Chapter Four
"THE HABITS OF THE LIFE"

WEEK FIVE

DAY ONE

Prayer
Lord, I want to be changed, but I don't like the process, especially because it involves some kind of pain. Give me power beyond my own will to help me remain in the pain while You walk with me through my transformation.

Today's Reading
Choose the Life, chapter 4 (page 61 through page 64, paragraph 2)

Questions
1. Why should we practice the spiritual disciplines?

2. How do "habits create character"?

Reflection
What do you consider to be your best habit? What would others consider to be your worst habit? How did you develop these habits?

Prayer
Pray for each member of your Community and their shared requests.

DAY TWO

Prayer
Lord, I've tried and tried so many times to make the "right" changes in myself. I know that I am at war with myself—that as strong is my will is to change, the same strength of my will is opposing that change, desiring to remain the same. Lord, please rescue me from my "body of death." Create in me *one* will: Yours.

Today's Reading
Choose the Life, chapter 4 (page 64, paragraph 3, through page 66)

Questions
1. What is meant by "Spiritual disciplines are to transformation what calisthenics are to sport"?

2. What does it mean that the spiritual disciplines have to "work indirectly" in creating character?

Reflection
Why is willpower alone of little help in our transformation?

Prayer
Pray for each member of your Community and their shared requests.

DAY THREE

Prayer
Lord, I've worked hard to know more about You. I now desire to be the kind of person You are delighted to know. Help me become that kind of person: Your friend.

Today's Reading
Choose the Life, chapter 4 (page 67 through page 69, paragraph 2)

Questions
1. What was meant by the claim that "grace is not opposed to effort; it is opposed to earning"? Do you agree with this claim? Why or why not?

2. What is the "malpractice of the disciplines"?

Reflection
What do each of the tools (spiritual disciplines) in your "tool shed" look like? Which ones are well worn from constant use? Which ones are rusty? Which ones have never been taken out of their packages? Which ones are neglected because you aren't sure you know what they are for or how to use them?

Prayer
Pray for each member of your Community and their shared requests.

DAY FOUR

Prayer
Lord, I confess that I have been one of the "undisciplined disciples." I choose now a different life. I will no longer try to be godly; I will train to be godly. I choose Your life.

Today's Reading
Choose the Life, chapter 4 (page 69, paragraph 3, through page 74, paragraph 2)

Questions
1. What is an "undisciplined disciple"?

2. What is the "cost of non-discipleship"?

Reflection
What has "non-discipleship" cost you personally?

Prayer
Pray for each member of your Community and their shared requests.

DAY FIVE

Prayer
Lord, I've found it hard to follow You, not because I do not know the right thing to do (I usually do) but because it's easier (almost automatic) to do otherwise. My "default setting" is usually set to responding differently from what I know is the right response. Please train me so that I will respond freely and easily from a different default setting: Yours.

Today's Reading
Choose the Life, chapter 4 (page 74, paragraph 3, through page 79)

Questions
1. What is the "power of habit"?

2. Discuss the difference in attitude between "trying" and "training" to be godly?

Reflection
How is it that training in the spiritual disciplines causes Jesus' yoke to be "easy" (Matthew 11:30)?

Prayer
Pray for each member of your Community and their shared requests.

Choose the Life, **Chapter Four**
"THE HABITS OF THE LIFE"

WEEK FIVE

Community Meeting

DAY SIX

In preparation for this week's Meeting, you will have read chapter 4, "The Habits of the Life," in *Choose the Life* and have answered the reading questions for each day.

As a group, answer the following questions.

Questions
1. Drawing from the disciplines listed in the introductory paragraph, which ones have you engaged in at one time or another? (You may discover that you have experienced most of them.) At that time, what effect did they have upon you?

2. Looking again at the list. Write down examples of these disciplines being practiced in the life of Jesus.

The Spiritual Discipline	Jesus Practicing That Discipline

Reflection
1. Training to practice the spiritual disciplines without being held accountable is very difficult. What are the challenges you face in connecting at a deep level with another person or small group (keeping in mind that some of the necessary qualities to cultivate a helpful relationship are humility, submission, and vulnerability)?

2. Knowing that not all the spiritual disciplines are to be practiced concurrently, how will you decide which ones should be practiced when? Which ones have you determined are crucial for you to practice at this time?

Close
Share matters for the Community to pray about throughout the following week. Pray to close the meeting.

> *The spiritual disciplines transform the mind and train us for everything. . . . Character is formed by the Holy Spirit, and the disciplines are the tools.*

> *Choose the Life*, **Chapter Five**
> **"THE INNER WORKINGS OF THE LIFE"**

WEEK SIX

DAY ONE

Prayer
Lord, when I was young, I had many visions of being great. But as I grew older, I realized (for whatever reason) that almost all of my visions would not come true. Yet, even with this disappointment, I still have that hunger inside me to be in some way uniquely great. Lord, help me to become the uniquely great person You have always meant me to be.

Today's Reading
Choose the Life, chapter 5 (page 81 through page 85, paragraph 1)

Question
What good can having a positive vision of yourself when you are young do for you in the future?

Reflection
What part does vision play in your spiritual formation?

Prayer
Pray for each member of your Community and their shared requests.

DAY TWO

Prayer
Lord, I know that You have *accepted* me "just as I am," but I know also that You will never be *satisfied* with me as such. Teach me to be dissatisfied with who I have been and train me to prefer being the new person You are making.

Today's Reading
Choose the Life, chapter 5 (page 85, paragraph 2, through page 89, paragraph 3)

Questions
1. Why is being crucified with Christ the necessary step to taking on a new spiritual person?

2. What does subjecting the will have to do with triggering transformation?

Reflection
Transformation is a process. What are some specific steps you are taking to balance the passive voice (see Romans 6:6–8) of the Christian faith and the active voice (see Galatians 5:24–5) — in other words, the *being* and the *doing*?

Prayer
Pray for each member of your Community and their shared requests.

DAY THREE

Prayer
Lord, You know that I'm not very comfortable with "sharing" and discussing my personal thoughts and ideas and feelings with others. Please help me to be concerned with becoming who You want me to be rather than with what other's think about who I am now.

Today's Reading
Choose the Life, chapter 5 (page 89, paragraph 4, through page 91)

Questions
1. How is "learning to live in the disciplines . . . similar to learning a foreign language"?

2. In what ways are commitment and involvement in a discipleship community essential to transformation?

Reflection
What is it about commitment and involvement in a discipleship community that you find positive, or negative, or just worrisome?

Prayer
Pray for each member of your Community and their shared requests.

DAY FOUR

Prayer
Lord, teach me about how You intend to change me. I know from my own experience that just changing my mind about something usually doesn't change anything else about me. Help me to learn how to change.

Today's Reading
Choose the Life, chapter 5 (page 92 through page 96, paragraph 1)

Questions
1. What does the author mean when he states that "the body is a tool for God"? Does God mean to use our bodies to transform the other "parts" of us? How? (Consider Romans 12:1-2.)

2. How is transformation both an "inside-out" and an "outside-in" operation?

Reflection
What natural circumstances of life has God used as opportunities to grow you to be like Him?

Prayer
Pray for each member of your Community and their shared requests.

DAY FIVE

Prayer
Lord, I'm coming to believe that You really are dedicated to making me into all I can be. All I ask is for You to be with me when it gets tough.

Today's Reading
Choose the Life, chapter 5 (page 96, paragraph 2, through page 100)

Questions
1. What were the two events or experiences that were reported to have caused the most important spiritual transformation?

2. What does it tell you about God's determination to grow you to complete maturity when He will use even our feelings of being "utterly, unbearably crushed" and "despairing of life" to form us?

Reflection
What fears keep you from following Jesus fully?

Prayer
Pray for each member of your Community and their shared requests.

> *Choose the Life*, **Chapter Five**
> **"THE INNER WORKINGS OF THE LIFE"**

WEEK SIX

Community Meeting

DAY SIX

In preparation for this week's Meeting, you will have read chapter 5, "The Inner Workings of the Life," in *Choose the Life* and have answered the reading questions for each day.

As a group, answer the following questions.

Questions

1. What was your vision of your future when you were young? Did you have an alter ego like the author's Bobby Logan?

2. Talk about the difference between the first and second crucifixion in practical terms (the difference between the passive voice [the first crucifixion] and the active voice [the second crucifixion]).

Reflection
What are some ways God has used transformational combinations in your life?

Close
Share matters for the Community to pray about throughout the following week. Pray to close the meeting.

Following Jesus . . . requires a different value system. He is to lead, and I am to follow, which means I give up the right to run my own life.

Choose the Life, Chapter Six
"THE MIND AND THE LIFE"

WEEK SEVEN

DAY ONE

Prayer
Lord, I understand that many things untrue, unhealthy, and undesirable to You find a home in my mind. Train me, Lord, to make my mind a place that is inhospitable to any thought that opposes You.

Today's Reading
Choose the Life, chapter 6 (page 101 through page 107, paragraph 2)

Questions
1. What does Paul mean by telling us that we need Christ's "attitude" or "mind-set" in us?

2. How can the mind be reprogrammed?

Reflection
Why is it sometimes difficult to accept as true something that you have believed to be false, even when you fully agree that the facts in evidence are irrefutable and compelling? Give an example.

Prayer
Pray for each member of your Community and their shared requests.

DAY TWO

Prayer
Lord, I need to be trained to recognize Your voice. I know that I have to move from speaking about You to letting You speak within me, from thinking about You to letting You think within me, from acting for and with You to letting You act through me.

Today's Reading
Choose the Life, chapter 6 (page 107, paragraph 3, through page 111)

Questions
1. What are some false ideas that God has changed in your thinking?

2. What, according to the author, is the basic message in all temptation?

Reflection
What are some good ways to detect those false beliefs that have become resident in your mind that you use unconsciously in your thinking?

Prayer
Pray for each member of your Community and their shared requests.

DAY THREE

Prayer
Lord, lead me not in my temptation, but deliver me from the Evil One.

Today's Reading
Choose the Life, chapter 6 (page 112 through page 116, paragraph 1)

Questions
1. What are some of "Satan's favorite ideas"?

2. What in your beliefs are each of the "ideas" aimed at attacking?

Reflection
How does your struggle with insecurity describe what you truly believe about what God is really like?

Prayer
Pray for each member of your Community and their shared requests.

DAY FOUR

Prayer
Lord, what lies have I believed? What images of myself and others are distorted? Lord, bring down those strongholds.

Today's Reading
Choose the Life, chapter 6 (page 116, paragraph 1, through page 122, paragraph 1)

Questions
1. How can what you see in the mirror (your self-image) affect the way you live your life?

2. What did Tozer mean by "Whatever comes into your mind when you think about God is the most important thing about you"?

Reflection
What strategy can you use to "take every idea and image captive" under the control of the Spirit working in you?

Prayer
Pray for each member of your Community and their shared requests.

DAY FIVE

Prayer
Lord, let my mind and its ideas, images, and feelings be purified through the washing of the Word. Direct my repentance, and lead me to be fully healthy so that I can love You with all my heart, soul, mind, and strength.

Today's Reading
Choose the Life, chapter 6 (page 122, paragraph 1, through page 126)

Questions
1. Describe how "feelings are the product of both" ideas and images?

2. What is meant by "Passions and desires (also known as feelings) are the most used and powerful tools that trigger sinful actions"?

Reflection
What is the relationship between "feelings," "repentance," and "health"?

Prayer
Pray for each member of your Community and their shared requests.

> *Choose the Life*, **Chapter Six**
> **"THE MIND AND THE LIFE"**

WEEK SEVEN

Community Meeting

DAY SIX

In preparation for this week's Meeting, you will have read chapter 6, "The Mind and the Life," in *Choose the Life* and have answered the reading questions for each day.

As a group, answer the following questions.

Questions

1. Briefly recount a recent conversation you've had with a person of a completely different worldview from your own. Was it difficult for you to "get through" to the person? Why or why not?

2. What are "strongholds"? How do we get them? How do we get loose from them?

Reflection
1. Have there been moments when you were the "deeply loved, secure disciple" who was inspired by God's love to take a risk? Share the experience with your group.

2. Take twenty minutes and have each person practice Madame Guyon's method for meditation on Scripture. Use 1 Corinthians 9:24-27. Describe the experience to the group.

Close
Share matters for the Community to pray about throughout the following week. Pray to close the meeting.

> *Waiting on God is not waiting around; it is actively persevering in obedience as we wait for God to orchestrate circumstances.*

Choose the Life, **Chapter Seven**
"RELATIONSHIPS AND THE LIFE"

WEEK EIGHT

DAY ONE

Prayer
Lord, I've always thought that You gave me skill by which I should lead people. Teach me how to lead from my character.

Today's Reading
Choose the Life, chapter 7 (page 127 through page 129, paragraph 3)

Question
What are the perils of leading from your competence?

Reflection
Recount a time when your skills were not sufficient to properly accomplish something that just had to be done right (and right then). What did you think about yourself when your skills "failed" you?

Prayer
Pray for each member of your Community and their shared requests.

DAY TWO

Prayer
Lord, I desire to grow in Your grace. Grow me into someone You would be comfortable with entrusting the growth of Your other children.

Today's Reading
Choose the Life, chapter 7 (page 129, paragraph 4, through page 134, paragraph 1)

Questions
1. What is meant by "the disciple-making climate"? What is the current "disciple-making climate" like?

2. What do "relationships of trust" and "environments of grace" look like?

Reflection
Why do you think a proper balance of relationships, principles, and environment is so difficult to establish and maintain?

Prayer
Pray for each member of your Community and their shared requests.

DAY THREE

Prayer
Lord, I've heard about Your strength being made perfect in my weakness, but I must say I do not desire to be seen as weak. Please help me to understand the defect in my thoughts and desires.

Today's Reading
Choose the Life, chapter 7 (page 134, paragraph 1, through page 141, paragraph 4)

Questions
1. What are the "Capacity" and the "Character" ladders? What do they indicate?

2. Why will being higher on the "Character" ladder take you further than being high on the "Capacity" ladder?

Reflection
How have you relied more on "Capacity" than "Character"?

Prayer
Pray for each member of your Community and their shared requests.

DAY FOUR

Prayer
Lord, I am so sorry for having been any part of dragging someone down who is enjoying Your blessings. Teach me to be mindful that I am to be Your instrument of blessing to build others up, not an instrument of the Evil One causing Your little ones to stumble.

Today's Reading
Choose the Life, chapter 7 (page 141, paragraph 5, through page 149, paragraph 2)

Questions
1. What are "relationships of trust"?

2. How does the "ladder of success" relate to "relationships of trust"?

Reflection
Relate an experience in which you were brought crashing down from a glorious spiritual success by people who should not have done so. What would have had to be different to have kept this experience from happening?

Prayer
Pray for each member of your Community and their shared requests.

DAY FIVE

Prayer
Lord, help me to remember the great patience You show to me as I train to be godly. Bring to my memory the many times You have responded to my failings and my incompetence with graciousness. Your grace inspires me to move beyond my own vision.

Today's Reading
Choose the Life, chapter 7 (page 149, paragraph 3, through page 156)

Questions
1. What is an "environment of grace"?

2. How does the "ladder of success" relate to "environments of grace"?

Reflection
How do you react when you are affirmed by others? What does it motivate you to do? Do you agree that "it arouses the desire to please God"?

Prayer
Pray for each member of your Community and their shared requests.

> *Choose the Life*, **Chapter Seven**
> **"RELATIONSHIPS AND THE LIFE"**

WEEK EIGHT

Community Meeting

DAY SIX

In preparation for this week's Meeting, you will have read chapter 7, "Relationships and the Life," in *Choose the Life* and have answered the reading questions for each day.

As a group, answer the following questions.

Questions
1. Describe a relationship of trust (page 146).

2. Describe an environment of grace (page 149).

Reflection
1. There are three elements to the discipleship climate: principles, relationships, and environment. Review the author's story and describe what was working or not working in his environment (pages 130–154).

2. The author talks about how competency took him just so far and then let him down. Why do you think he thought competency was enough (pages 134–136)?

Close
Share matters for the Community to pray about throughout the following week. Pray to close the meeting.

> *The ideas that need to be transformed are deeply embedded, and so the Scriptures will need to go just as deep. . . . It is an acquired skill to go deep, to reroute the words through the heart in prayer and reflection.*

> *Choose the Life*, **Chapter Eight**
> **"SUBMISSION AND THE LIFE"**

WEEK NINE

DAY ONE

Prayer
Lord, I confess that the first indicator that I'm being successful is the accolades I receive from people with whom I work. I love to be praised, and then I act humble. Train me to love being Your blessing to others, especially when my service is unknown to them.

Today's Reading
Choose the Life, chapter 8 (page 157 through page 162, paragraph 1)

Questions
1. The author claims that Jesus' core character trait was "humility, which manifested itself in submission"—that this is "the heart of Jesus' life and mission; everything else flows from it." Explain why this is true (or false).

2. What justifies Nouwen's statement that "the Christian leader of the future is called to be completely irrelevant and to stand in this world with nothing to offer but his or her own vulnerable self"?

Reflection
R. Scott Rodin said, "When our daily self-worth and the measure of our effectiveness come primarily from the reaction of those with whom we work, then we are finished as Christian leaders." Why do you think he believes this to be true? By what means do you measure your self-worth and effectiveness?

Prayer
Pray for each member of your Community and their shared requests.

DAY TWO

Prayer
Lord, I fear being insignificant. I've always tried to make sure what I do would count for something. I've never really stopped to ask myself who is doing the counting? I now realize that for me to follow You, I must let You do the counting. Lord, train me to live by Your standards, Your system of "weights and measures."

Today's Reading
Choose the Life, chapter 8 (page 162, paragraph 2, through page 166, paragraph 1)

Questions
1. What is it that is "in a man" that makes him untrustworthy?

2. According to Jesus' culture, in what ways was He "irrelevant"?

Reflection
Describe the freedom you would have if, according to your culture, you were "irrelevant"?

Prayer
Pray for each member of your Community and their shared requests.

DAY THREE

Prayer
Lord, train me to behave as though I really do believe the extent to which You love and value me.

Today's Reading
Choose the Life, chapter 8 (page 166, paragraph 1, through page 168, paragraph 3)

Questions
1. How does humility cure our need for false identity?

2. What is meant by "Submission to mission is the cornerstone of humility, of living in the light of who God says we are"?

Reflection
How would you be different if you really did believe the extent to which God loves and values you? What would you fear? What would limit you?

Prayer
Pray for each member of your Community and their shared requests.

DAY FOUR

Prayer
Lord, there are times when it's gotten so tough that I've given up. I want to be someone You can count on. What will it take to become a disciple that will endure to the end?

Today's Reading
Choose the Life, chapter 8 (page 168, paragraph 4, through page 172, paragraph 3)

Questions
1. What does it mean that "submission is a love word before it is an authority word"?

2. How will true humility sustain us through the tough times?

Reflection
Describe a time when you have been abandoned, left alone to continue on your own. What kept you going? Or, if you stopped, what caused you to throw in the towel?

Prayer
Pray for each member of your Community and their shared requests.

DAY FIVE

Prayer
Lord, who is it that You want to affirm through me today? Who is it that you wish for me to remind that they are very valuable to You?

Today's Reading
Choose the Life, chapter 8 (page 172, paragraph 4, through page 178)

Questions
1. What are three things that the submissive life affords us?

2. What was the problem with Timothy that Paul was addressing when he advised him to "fan into flames" the gift of God that was within him? Why was this advice excellent counsel?

Reflection
Who needs your affirmation, a reminder of their value to God? Give it today!

Prayer
Pray for each member of your Community and their shared requests.

> *Choose the Life*, **Chapter Eight**
> **"SUBMISSION AND THE LIFE"**

WEEK NINE

Community Meeting

DAY SIX

In preparation for this week's Meeting, you will have read chapter 8, "Submission and the Life," in *Choose the Life* and have answered the reading questions for each day.

As a group, answer the following questions.

Questions
1. What is the most compelling reason to live a life of submission (page 156, see Richard Foster's statement)?

2. Talk about how the following results happen when we live in submission to one another?
   - Our needs are met
   - We will develop humility
   - Others are free to love us
     (meaning that I allow their gifts and care to be applied to my life, because I am open and vulnerable before them)

Reflection

Write out an affirmation statement about someone in your life or in the group. Make it in the tradition of Paul's affirmation of Timothy. Share it with that person or the group.

Close

Share matters for the Community to pray about throughout the following week. Pray to close the meeting.

> *When leaders model and communicate authentic relationships, it is a powerful tool for God to use.*

> *Choose the Life*, Chapter Nine
> "LEADERSHIP AND THE LIFE"

WEEK TEN

DAY ONE

Prayer
Lord, I sometimes have been critical of Your church, forgetting that I have never really seen it as You see it: in all its power and glory. I repent of placing myself above what You love so dearly.

Today's Reading
Choose the Life, chapter 9 (pages 179–188)

Questions
1. What does the author mean when he describes the church as "always vacillating between glory and the grotesque"?

2. What do the trap leaders find themselves in, and how can they get out of it (pages 180–185)?

Reflection
What are some temptations leaders face when trying to live by the same principles that Jesus lived by?

Prayer
Pray for each member of your Community and their shared requests.

DAY TWO

Prayer
Lord, I've always considered being irrelevant and unnecessary as bad things. Teach me why You want me to be them.

Today's Reading
Choose the Life, chapter 9 (page 189 through page 196, paragraph 1)

Questions
1. What does it mean to be "irrelevant" and "unnecessary" (pages 184–188)?

2. Does being "irrelevant" and "unnecessary" imply that we must ignore and withdraw from the culture in which we live?

Reflection
How can attendance at religious services be understood in a balanced way (note the statements by Trueblood and Willard, pages 189–191)?

Prayer
Pray for each member of your Community and their shared requests.

DAY THREE

Prayer
Lord, I know that Your love for me overflows out of the abundance of Your heart. I also know that I cannot give what I do not have. Train me to love from a satisfied soul.

Today's Reading
Choose the Life, chapter 9 (page 196, paragraph 2, through page 211, paragraph 1)

Questions
1. Why practice the spiritual disciplines of silence and solitude?

2. Describe what you think a satisfied soul is (based on Psalm 23).

Reflection
How would your actions be different if you lived from a fully satisfied soul?

Prayer
Pray for each member of your Community and their shared requests.

DAY FOUR

Prayer
Lord, train me to trust in Your ways, especially when my culture tells me You are mistaken.

Today's Reading
Choose the Life, chapter 9 (page 211, paragraph 2, through page 216, paragraph 1)

Questions
1. Describe what others would see if you gave yourself to the principle of discipleship.

2. According to Trueblood, what is "one of the most powerful ways of turning people's loyalty to Christ"? Why is this way so powerful?

Reflection
Why do we leaders (and you in particular) tend to ignore the second of the Greatest Commandments (loving our neighbor), preferring the latest technique for church growth/evangelism?

Prayer
Pray for each member of your Community and their shared requests.

DAY FIVE

Prayer
Lord, my desire is to know You through whatever means You deem best for me at this time. Please grow in me the willingness to discover You through means with which I may not be familiar.

Today's Reading
Choose the Life, chapter 9 (page 216, paragraph 2, through page 221)

Questions
1. How does the author suggest we prepare to give ourselves to others?

2. What is *lectio divina*? What will this process do?

Reflection
Using the process called *lectio divina*, interact with God through His Word. Describe your encounter.

Prayer
Pray for each member of your Community and their shared requests.

> *Choose the Life*, **Chapter Nine**
> **"LEADERSHIP AND THE LIFE"**

WEEK TEN

Community Meeting

DAY SIX

In preparation for this week's Meeting, you will have read chapter 9, "Leadership and the Life," in *Choose the Life* and have answered the reading questions for each day.

As a group, answer the following questions.

Question
How does our (Western) culture militate against the values that Jesus modeled?

Reflection
1. Identify a few ways in which the prevailing culture has affected you. Discuss the way you use your money and the material things you buy. In other words, what is driving you? Are your goals related to meeting the needs for relevance according to the world's values?

2. How has the experience with *Choose the Life* caused you to make changes in your behavior?

Close
Share matters for the Community to pray about throughout the following week. Pray to close the meeting.

> *Our radical nature is expressed in our stubborn insistence that we follow the humility and submission of Jesus in His agenda and ways of touching others. What can be done with competence alone is puny and meager compared to a life that is lived out of the character of Christ in us.*

APPENDIX

Choose the Life Community Purpose and Covenant

Our Community's Purpose Is:
To develop relationships with one another that will help, support, and encourage each of us to grow in Christlikeness through loving one another by sharing our thoughts, experiences, concerns, fears, successes, and failures and by serving one another when a need or the opportunity arises as we choose the life and explore a faith that embraces discipleship.

Therefore, I commit, for the next ten weeks to accomplishing our purpose by:

- Making my spiritual growth and relationship with God one of my top three priorities (with spouse and family)
- Completing the daily readings and exercises on time, each week, according to the *Guide*
- Being faithful in my attendance to Community Meetings (only injury, sickness, family, and work schedule conflicts are reasonable excuses for absences) and calling prior to the weekly meeting to inform our leader of my absence
- Participating in discussion, prayer, and the sharing of ideas
- Being honest and open when I share my thoughts and feelings
- Maintaining complete confidentiality of anything discussed in our group by our members (unless prior permission to disclose the information has been given by all individuals involved)
- Praying daily for each member of the Community and the needs they have shared

Name: _____

Date: _____

LEADER'S GUIDE

WEEK 1

Your First Community Meeting

In preparation for this meeting, all Community members will have read Dallas Willard's foreword (pages 6–8) and preface, "A Conversation Starter" (pages 9–14), from *Choose the Life* and have written their answers to each of the questions posed in the *Guide* for the first week's Community Meeting.

At This Week's Introductory Meeting
1. Open with prayer, asking the Lord to help you become conscious of any difference that may exist between what He means by discipleship and what we have allowed it to become. Pray that He will grow in us the desire to be obedient as we live out His faith.
2. Play the introductory video clip "Cheap Grace" from the DVD guide to *Choose the Life*.
3. Collect the signed Choose the Life Community Purpose and Covenant from each Community member.
4. Read aloud the following introduction to this week's meeting:

Dallas Willard begins his foreword to *Choose the Life* with, "There are now signs that significant groups among professing Christians are ready to take up discipleship to Jesus as the core of their religious life." One of those signs is your reading *Choose the Life* and your participation in a Community that will discuss the core thoughts and key ideas and apply the practices presented therein. The use of the word *core* indicates that it is central to one's life. The following discussion is designed to draw out a person's spiritual readiness to choose the life of following Jesus—a life of humility, obedience, submission, and sacrifice.

5. Discuss with the members of your Community the answers you came up with for this week's questions.

Questions
1. When you were a child, to what were you highly committed? Describe what that commitment entailed and how it affected your commitments as an adult.

2. Dallas Willard cites three things vital to spiritual growth (pages 6–7). Discuss each one and evaluate its place in your present experience.

3. What does Bonhoeffer mean by "cheap grace" (page 10)? Do you think "cheap grace" is a problem in your life, faith community, or church? How is it manifested?

4. Do you agree with the description of the "problem" and the "solution" advanced (pages 11–13)?

Reflection
Talk with one another about your readiness (or reluctance), at this time, to choose the life — specifically, about living out "a faith that embraces discipleship." Why now?

Prayer
Share matters for the Community to pray about throughout the following week. Make note of the requests made to use in your daily time of prayer.

Close
Pray together to close the meeting.

WEEK TWO

Community Meeting

DAY SIX

In preparation for this week's Meeting, you will have read chapter 1, "How I Got to This Point," in *Choose the Life* and have answered the reading questions for each day.

At This Week's Meeting
1. Open this session by asking God to help you "be transformed from relevance to prayer, from popularity to ministry, and from leading to being lead." Ask Him to help you "jump in" and swim the "uncertain seas of downward mobility."
2. Play video clip 2, "How I got to this Point."
3. Read aloud the following introduction to this week's Meeting:

> Most of us don't willingly invite change into our lives. I suppose one exception to that rule is getting something we really want that is shiny and new: a car, a house, a trip, a new spouse. Generally, however, we resist change. In fact, the cause of every problem is change. Change is painful; change threatens our safety and security, and it makes us less confident of our abilities. When that change challenges one's very sense of identity, it intimidates and is naturally resisted. But if we want to grow in the image of Christ, change is the name of the game. Transformation is change, and that change comes only when we say, "Lord, I'm not afraid of any change You want to make in my life." It is to this destination that we go in this lesson.

As a group, answer the following questions.

Questions
1. What did the author mean when he used the metaphor of "fly-fishing on ice" to represent his struggles while serving as senior pastor at a "successful" church?

2. What are the differences between believing in Jesus and believing what Jesus believed (pages 19–20)?

Discuss the fivefold way the author presents of how we are to follow Jesus (pages 19–20).

Reflection
1. What are we to understand by the author's statement that "competence is a cul-de-sac"?

2. How are brokenness and humility "essential to spiritual health"?

Close

Share matters for the Community to pray about throughout the following week. Pray to close the meeting.

> *Jesus calls us not to sin management but to transformation, where we experience one breakthrough after another and do away with sin in our lives.*

WEEK THREE

Community Meeting

DAY SIX

In preparation for this week's Meeting, you will have read chapter 2, "The Need for the Life," in *Choose the Life* and have answered the reading questions for each day.

At This Week's Meeting
1. Open this session by praying for God to help us understand what it is about us that needs to be changed, to help us submit to however He intends to change us, to help us not to fear the repercussions of these changes, and to help us trust ourselves with Him.
2. Play video clip 3, "The Need for the Life."
3. Read aloud the following introduction to this week's Meeting:

> There is common concern among church watchers that the message has been compromised and the harmful results have cascaded down into our definition of faith and what it means to be a Christian. The test for salvation has become doctrinal rather than behavioral. We have ritualized salvation with walking the aisle, praying to receive Christ, or signing a doctrinal statement. The trouble with our evangelism is that we have made it so easy to enter the Christian life that we miss the repentance, commitment, and regeneration that provide the power to live the Christian life. The trouble with our discipleship is that it is "in-house" and non-reproductive. These two factors alone account for not only the decline in church attendance but also, more important, the decline in disciples being "salt and light" in the world.

As a group, answer the following questions.

Questions
1. Discuss whether your test for salvation has been primarily "doctrinal" rather than "behavioral."

2. Discuss the statement that "faith is only real in obedience." How does it challenge our modern notion of faith (page 24)?

3. How does holding a faith that does not transform lead to "sin management" (page 26)?

Reflection
Do you think your church and other churches have accepted a non-discipleship Christianity? Is it optional in your life? Do you think you have a choice (pages 26–30)?

Close
Share matters for the Community to pray about throughout the following week. Pray to close the meeting.

> *Discipleship today must also begin with a commitment of submission to at least one other person. Choosing the life begins right here.*

WEEK FOUR

Community Meeting

DAY SIX

In preparation for this week's Meeting, you will have read chapter 3, "The Call to the Life," in *Choose the Life* and have answered the reading questions for each day.

At This Week's Meeting
1. Open this session by praying for God to teach you how to hold your lives loosely, to become self-forgetting, and to lose yourselves in the joy of accomplishing His mission.
2. Play video clip 4, "The Call to the Life."
3. Read aloud the following introduction to this week's Meeting:

> It has been taught and caught in far too many Christian settings that Jesus' invitation, "If anyone would come after me, let him deny himself, take up his cross daily, and follow after Me," is for the spiritual elite—for those called to suffer, for those whom history will call "the saints." This idea leads us to the belief that there are a few chosen ones whose destiny is to live at a higher level than the rest of us and that it is the role of the ordinary disciple to support the special ones. While there may, by necessity, be an element of this in any group of people, Jesus' call is universal. This is why He uses the word *anyone*. The call to this kind of life is for everyone.
>
> As a group, answer the following questions.

Questions

1. What is meant by "Faith is more than agreement; it is taking up your cross"?

2. The author presents various things disciples are urged to follow. These alternatives to Jesus' calling may appeal to us but can be very dangerous. What are these alternatives, and why could they lead us astray (page 46)?

Reflection

1. How should a disciple give these alternatives their proper consideration when seeking to follow Jesus' leading?

2. Why is self-denial "essential" (page 49-52)?

Close

Share matters for the Community to pray about throughout the following week. Pray to close the meeting.

> *Until we actually step out in obedience to Him, we can't experience the transformation of our character. As we follow Him, Jesus will reveal more about Himself and our mission day by day.*

WEEK FIVE

Community Meeting

DAY SIX

In preparation for this week's Meeting, you will have read chapter 4, "The Habits of the Life," in *Choose the Life* and have answered the reading questions for each day.

At This Week's Meeting
1. Open this session in prayer.
2. Play video clip 5, "The Habits of the Life."
3. Read aloud the following introduction to this week's Meeting:

> The spiritual disciplines are essential to the deliverance of human beings from the concrete power of sin. The interplay between discipline and disciple is not without importance. John Ortberg says, "Disciplined people can do the right thing at the right time in the right way for the right reason."[4] The practice of the disciplines develops habits of the heart that make a disciple more capable of answering the call of God on his or her life. It is equally important to understand that the disciplines are simply tools that God uses to cultivate a more intimate relationship with us. The disciplines are meditation, chastity, service, fasting, sacrifice, worship, simplicity, fellowship, frugality, submission, prayer, secrecy, confession, study, celebration, silence, solitude, and charity.

> As a group, answer the following questions.

Questions

1. Drawing from the disciplines listed in the introductory paragraph, which ones have you engaged in at one time or another? (You may discover that you have experienced most of them.) At that time, what effect did they have upon you?

2. Looking again at the list. Write down examples of these disciplines being practiced in the life of Jesus.

The Spiritual Discipline	Jesus Practicing That Discipline

Reflection

1. Training to practice the spiritual disciplines without being held accountable is very difficult. What are the challenges you face in connecting at a deep level with another person or small group (keeping in mind that some of the necessary qualities to cultivate a helpful relationship are humility, submission, and vulnerability)?

2. Knowing that not all the spiritual disciplines are to be practiced concurrently, how will you decide which ones should be practiced when? Which ones have you determined are crucial for you to practice at this time?

Close

Share matters for the Community to pray about throughout the following week. Pray to close the meeting.

> *The spiritual disciplines transform the mind and train us for everything. . . . Character is formed by the Holy Spirit, and the disciplines are the tools.*

WEEK SIX

Community Meeting

DAY SIX

In preparation for this week's Meeting, you will have read chapter 5, "The Inner Workings of the Life," in *Choose the Life* and have answered the reading questions for each day.

At This Week's Meeting
1. Open this session in prayer.
2. Play video clip 6, "The Inner Workings of the Life."
3. Read aloud the following introduction to this week's Meeting:

> How is character formed? What really goes on inside when we are being spiritually formed? This session addresses the inner workings of transformation. When one commits to Christ, the life of discipleship begins. Discipleship means "I am in a state of following Christ, and, therefore, I arrange my life around the practices of Jesus." Spiritual formation is the direct act of the Holy Spirit on the inner person. Discipleship is the choice. The inner person is formed by the practice of the disciplines when our vision is to become like Christ. That is why we can say that the Spirit of the disciplines is the Holy Spirit.
>
> As a group, answer the following questions.

Questions

1. What was your vision of your future when you were young? Did you have an alter ego like the author's Bobby Logan?

2. Talk about the difference between the first and second crucifixion in practical terms (the difference between the passive voice [the first crucifixion] and the active voice [the second crucifixion]).

Reflection

What are some ways God has used transformational combinations in your life?

Close

Share matters for the Community to pray about throughout the following week. Pray to close the meeting.

> *Following Jesus . . . requires a different value system. He is to lead, and I am to follow, which means I give up the right to run my own life.*

WEEK SEVEN

Community Meeting

DAY SIX

In preparation for this week's Meeting, you will have read chapter 6, "The Mind and the Life," in *Choose the Life* and have answered the reading questions for each day.

At This Week's Meeting
1. Open this session in prayer.
2. Play video clip 7, "The Mind and the Life."
3. Read aloud the following introduction to this week's Meeting:

The genesis of transformation is the process of renewing the mind. Our minds are wired in such a way that we have thoughts that create images, feelings, and perceptions. Even spontaneous, unconscious action is based on a cognitive memory that is fixed in the mind (which explains why every time I think of eating liver I immediately gag). When Olympic athletes win the gold medal, they often cry on the awards platform at the sound of their national anthem and the sight of their flag being raised. This is about the idea that they have done something wonderful in the name of their country. The idea is empowered by the image of the flag and the sound of the music; therefore, it creates a powerful emotion. Our minds work the same whether it is what we think about politics, our favorite team, the members of our family, or our deeply held religious beliefs. This is why the battle for the mind is the most important of all.

Images are the pictures in our mind's eye. They are concrete and often specific. The images that accompany our ideas make them more powerful. They are what the Lincoln Memorial is to liberty, what Lance Armstrong is to dedication, and what Elvis Presley is to self-indulgence. Just as images can be powerfully used for good, they can also magnify negatives. One's negative image of self can override clear thinking or any other force in life.

As a group, answer the following questions.

Questions

1. Briefly recount a recent conversation you've had with a person of a completely different worldview from your own. Was it difficult for you to "get through" to them? Why or why not?

2. What are "strongholds"? How do we get them? How do we get loose from them?

Reflection
1. Have there been moments when you were the "deeply loved, secure disciple" who was inspired by God's love to take a risk? Share the experience with your group.

2. Take twenty minutes and have each person practice Madame Guyon's method for meditation on Scripture. Use 1 Corinthians 9:24-27. Describe the experience to the group.

Close
Share matters for the Community to pray about throughout the following week. Pray to close the meeting.

Waiting on God is not waiting around; it is actively persevering in obedience as we wait for God to orchestrate circumstances.

WEEK EIGHT

Community Meeting

DAY SIX

In preparation for this week's Meeting, you will have read chapter 7, "Relationships and the Life," in *Choose the Life* and have answered the reading questions for each day.

At This Week's Meeting
1. Open this session in prayer.
2. Play video clip 8, "Relationships and the Life."
3. Read aloud the following introduction to this week's Meeting:

> Bill Thrall wrote, "To rise above and beyond your individual best, you need a certain kind of environment in which to live and work. Such an environment would nurture the integration of heart and hand, word and deed, spirituality and everyday life. It would nourish your relationship with God and kindle your connections with those around you. This environment and the relationships it spawns would help you become the kind of leader others want to follow."[5] The most important question anyone can ask and get an answer to in connection to others is, "Can I trust me with you?" In other words, can we be honest together, can we then submit to each other, and, finally, can we help each other keep our commitments to God?

As a group, answer the following questions.

Questions
1. Describe a relationship of trust (page 146).

2. Describe an environment of grace (page 149).

Reflection
1. There are three elements to the discipleship climate: principles, relationships, and environment. Review the author's story and describe what was working or not working in his environment (pages 130–154).

2. The author talks about how competency took him just so far and then let him down. Why do you think he thought competency was enough (pages 134–136)?

Close
Share matters for the Community to pray about throughout the following week. Pray to close the meeting.

> *The ideas that need to be transformed are deeply embedded, and so the Scriptures will need to go just as deep. . . . It is an acquired skill to go deep, to reroute the words through the heart in prayer and reflection.*

WEEK NINE

Community Meeting

DAY SIX

In preparation for this week's Meeting, you will have read chapter 8, "Submission and the Life," in *Choose the Life* and have answered the reading questions for each day.

At This Week's Meeting
1. Open this session in prayer.
2. Play video clip 9, "Submission and the Life."
3. Read aloud the following introduction to this week's Meeting:

> The greatest truth about submission is that we submit to what we trust. It is also true that most think of submission as a negative, as placing yourself in jeopardy; it conjures up images of abuse or of cult behavior. Americans are told never to give up their passport or rights as citizens. Jesus demonstrated that submission was the means His Father used to unleash His grace and mercy on the world. Jesus modeled giving up His rights and changed the world by leading with His weakness. This session teaches us that submission is a love word before it is an authority word. In fact, we will learn that unless we do submit to others we trust, we won't get our needs met; we will lack humility, and we will keep others from loving us.
>
> As a group, answer the following questions.

Questions

1. What is the most compelling reason to live a life of submission (page 156, see Richard Foster's statement)?

2. Talk about how the following results happen when we live in submission to one another?
   - Our needs are met
   - We will develop humility
   - Others are free to love us
     (meaning that I allow their gifts and care to be applied to my life, because I am open and vulnerable before them)

Reflection

Write out an affirmation statement about someone in your life or in the group. Make it in the tradition of Paul's affirmation of Timothy. Share it with that person or the group.

Close
Share matters for the Community to pray about throughout the following week. Pray to close the meeting.

When leaders model and communicate authentic relationships, it is a powerful tool for God to use.

WEEK TEN

Community Meeting

DAY SIX

In preparation for this week's Meeting, you will have read chapter 9, "Leadership and the Life," in *Choose the Life* and have answered the reading questions for each day.

At This Week's Meeting
1. Open this session in prayer.
2. Play video clip 10, "Leadership and the Life."
3. Read aloud the following introduction to this week's Meeting:

> Many leaders feel trapped, unable to do the work they are called to do because of working conditions. This is very common for teachers, professionals in the medical community, and those who practice law. It is also a big problem for religious leaders, both clergy and laity. The trap is real and many Christians find themselves in it. It is characterized by the desire to be relevant and the need to feel necessary.
>
> Getting off the gods of our religious culture to which we are addicted is like going through detox. Their allure is so strong that it might require beginning with a complete separation from the conditions in which we live. That means spending some extended time in solitude with others of like mind in order to reset your inner compass. The gods of attendance, progress, and competence plague all serious Christians. This session addresses the pathway out to a new way of being and doing.

As a group, answer the following questions.

Question
How does our (Western) culture militate against the values that Jesus modeled?

Reflection
1. Identify a few ways in which the prevailing culture has affected you. Discuss the way you use your money and the material things you buy. In other words, what is driving you? Are your goals related to meeting the needs for relevance according to the world's values?

2. How has the experience with *Choose the Life* caused you to make changes in your behavior?

Close

Share matters for the Community to pray about throughout the following week. Pray to close the meeting.

> *Our radical nature is expressed in our stubborn insistence that we follow the humility and submission of Jesus in his agenda and ways of touching others. What can be done with competence alone is puny and meager compared to a life that is lived out of the character of Christ in us.*

NOTES

1. Henri Nouwen, *In the Name of Jesus: Reflections on Christian Leadership* (New York: Crossroad, 1993), 60.
2. Dietrich Bonhoeffer, *The Cost of Discipleship* (New York: Macmillan, 1963), 63–64.
3. William Glasser, *Control Theory in the Classroom* (New York: Harper & Row, 1986); *Reality Therapy: A New Approach to Psychiatry* (New York: Harper & Row, 1965).
4. John Ortberg, *The Life You've Always Wanted: Spiritual Disciplines for Ordinary People* (Grand Rapids, MI: Zondervan, 1997), 54.
5. Bill Thrall, Bruce McNicol, and Ken McElrath, *The Ascent of a Leader: How Ordinary Relationships Develop Extraordinary Character and Influence* (San Francisco: Jossey-Bass, 1999), 1.

ABOUT THE AUTHORS

BILL HULL's mission is to call the church to return to its disciple-making roots. He is a writer and discipleship evangelist calling the church to *choose the life*, a journey that Jesus called every disciple to pursue. This journey leads to a life of spiritual transformation and service. A veteran pastor, Bill has written ten books on this subject. In 1990 he founded T-NET International, a ministry devoted to transforming churches into disciple-making churches.

The core of Bill's writing is *Jesus Christ, Disciplemaker*; *The Disciple-Making Pastor*; and *The Disciple-Making Church*. He now spends his time helping leaders experience personal transformation so they can help transform their churches.

Bill and his wife, Jane, enjoy their not-so-quiet life, helping to raise their "highly energetic" grandchildren, in the beautiful Southern California sunshine.

PAUL MASCARELLA has served in local church ministry for more than twenty-five years as an associate pastor, minister of music, and worship director while holding an executive management position at a daily newspaper in Los Angeles, California. He is associate director of *Choose the Life Ministries*, where the abundance of his time and energy go to assisting churches as they embark on The *Choose the Life Journey*, and proceed forward with the EXPERIENCE THE LIFE series. He also serves on the board of directors for Bill Hull Ministries. He holds the Bachelor of Philosophy and Master of Theological Studies degrees.

Paul and his wife, Denise, reside in Southern California.

OTHER BOOKS BY BILL HULL

Complete Book of Discipleship
Jesus Christ, Disciplemaker (20th Anniversary Edition)
Straight Talk on Spiritual Power
Revival That Reforms
Building High Commitment in a Low-Commitment World
New Century Disciplemaking
The Disciple-Making Pastor
The Disciple-Making Church
7 Steps to Transform Your Church
Anxious for Nothing

Become More Like Jesus with the
EXPERIENCE THE LIFE
Bible Study Series

A 30-week life-changing study series.

EXPERIENCE THE LIFE, a 30-week life changing series for groups, is composed of five books, each six weeks long. You'll learn how to read Scripture, think about what you read, pray over it, and live the Word of God to others.

Each study sold separately as a participant's guide, or buy the group leader's guide, which includes the study, a leader's guide, and DVD featuring Bill Hull.

Book 1: Believe as Jesus Believed – Transformed Mind
Book 2: Live as Jesus Lived – Transformed Character
Book 3: Love as Jesus Loved – Transformed Relationships
Book 4: Minister as Jesus Ministered – Transformed Service
Book 5: Lead as Jesus Lead – Transformed Influence

To order copies, call NavPress at **1-800-366-7788**, or log on to **www.NavPress.com**.

NAVPRESS
Discipleship Inside Out™

Also by Bill Hull

The Disciple-Making Pastor, rev. & exp. ed.

BakerBooks

The Disciple-Making Church, updated ed.

BakerBooks

Jesus Christ, Disciplemaker, 20th ann. ed.

BakerBooks

Choose the Life

BakerBooks

Building High Commitment in a Low-Commitment World

Revell

www.bakerpublishinggroup.com

Change from ordinary to Christlike.

Christlike
Bill Hull
978-1-60006-694-8

To make a difference in the world, we need to become different ourselves. The final determination of whether or not a person is becoming Christlike is how we act in daily life. Bill Hull in *Christlike* will show you how to change outward actions by inner transformation through uncomplicated obedience.

To order copies, call NavPress at 1-800-366-7788 or log on to www.navpress.com.

Discipleship Inside Out™

NavPress - A Ministry of The Navigators

Wherever you are in your spiritual journey, NavPress will help you grow.

The NavPress mission is to advance the calling of The Navigators by publishing life-transforming products that are biblically rooted, culturally relevant, and highly practical.

www.navpress.com   1-800-366-7788

NAVPRESS